Simple Machines

What Is a Wedge?

By Lloyd G. Douglas

Children's Press®
A Division of Scholastic Inc.
New York / Toronto / London / Auckland / Sydney
Mexico City / New Delhi / Hong Kong
Danbury, Connecticut

Photo Credits: Cover © Raymond Gehman/Corbis; pp. 5, 7, 9, 15, 17, 19, 21 (top left, bottom left, bottom right) by Maura B. McConnell; pp. 11, 13, 21 (top right) by Cindy Reiman
Contributing Editor: Jennifer Silate
Book Design: Mindy Liu

Library of Congress Cataloging-in-Publication Data

Douglas, Lloyd G.
What is a wedge? / by Lloyd G. Douglas.
     p. cm. -- (Simple machines)
   Includes index.
   ISBN 0-516-23965-1 (library binding) -- ISBN 0-516-24026-9 (paperback)
   1. Wedges--Juvenile literature. I. Title.

TJ1201.W44 D68 2002
621.8'11--dc21

                                                         2002001411

Contents

This is a **wedge**.

A wedge is an object with at least one **sloped** side.

5

An **ax** is a wedge.

Both sides of the ax's blade are sloped.

The **edge** of the ax is sharp.

An ax is used to split wood apart.

A **chisel** is also a wedge.

11

A chisel is used to cut or chip things.

It can be used to chip wood.

13

Wedges are also used to stop things from moving.

This wedge is used to keep the car's tire from moving.

A **doorstop** is a wedge, too.

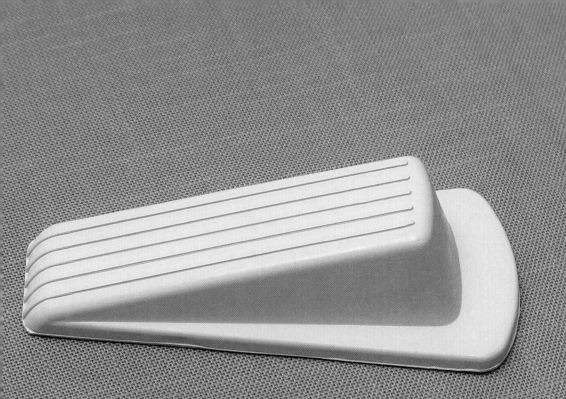

The doorstop keeps the door from closing.

Wedges have many different uses.

They are helpful **simple machines**.

21

New Words

ax (**aks**) a tool with a sharp blade on the end of a handle; used for chopping wood

chisel (**chiz**-uhl) a tool with a flat, sharp end used to cut or shape wood, stone, or metal

doorstop (**dor**-stop) a wedge used to keep doors from closing

edge (**ej**) the sharp side of a cutting tool

simple machines (**sihm**-puhl muh-**sheenz**) basic mechanical devices that make work easier

sloped (**slohpt**) at an angle, not straight

wedge (**wej**) an object with at least one sloped side

To Find Out More

Books
The Wedge
by Patricia Armentrout
The Rourke Book Company

What Are Wedges?
by Helen Frost
Pebble Books

Web Site
Spotlight on Simple Machines
http://sln.fi.edu/qa97/spotlight3/spotlight3.html
This Web site has lots of information about wedges and the other simple machines.

Index

About the Author

Lloyd G. Douglas is an editor and writer of children's books.

Reading Consultants

Kris Flynn, Coordinator, Small School District Literacy, The San Diego County Office of Education

Shelly Forys, Certified Reading Recovery Specialist, W.J. Zahnow Elementary School, Waterloo, IL

Sue McAdams, Former President of the North Texas Reading Council of the IRA, and Early Literacy Consultant, Dallas, TX